**More** Country Music for Laughin', Lovin' and Livin' It Up

(Another 510 Lines from Country Songs that may Someday be Written)

By

M. Gene Newport

authorHOUSE

1663 LIBERTY DRIVE, SUITE 200
BLOOMINGTON, INDIANA 47403
(800) 839-8640
WWW.AUTHORHOUSE.COM

© 2004 M. Gene Newport. All Rights Reserved.

No part of this book may be reproduced, stored in a retrieval system, or transmitted by any means without the written permission of the author.

First published by AuthorHouse 01/27/05

ISBN: 1-4208-1886-4 (sc)

Printed in the United States of America
Bloomington, Indiana

This book is printed on acid-free paper.

TABLE OF CONTENTS

THE UPS, DOWNS, OVERS AND UNDERS OF LOVE 1

TEARS, BEERS, BARS AND DRINKIN' 9

WHO'S LEAVIN' AND WHO'S COMIN' BACK? 13

THE EYES HAVE IT, DARLIN' 19

SO, WHAT DO YOU THINK OF ME? 25

PAY ATTENTION TO WHAT I'M TELLIN' YOU, DARLIN' 31

BEIN' SMART, BUT LOOKIN' DUMB 41

THE BARNYARD, THE CIRCUS AND THE ZOO 47

TRUCKS, TRAINS, JAILS AND PRISONS 53

SLEEPIN', DAY-DREAMIN' AND MAKIN' BELIEVE 55

WHAT YOU SEE AIN'T ALWAYS WHAT YOU GET 59

ACHES, PAINS, LOSSES AND GAINS 69

HUNTIN', FISHIN' AND YOU 79

GROWIN' UP, GROWIN' OUT AND GROWIN' SMARTER 81

LOVE, LOVE, LOVE 87

LAUGHIN', LOVIN' AND LIVIN' IT UP 97

IT'S EITHER TOO HOT OR TOO COLD 101

THERE'S BEEN A CHANGE
OF DIRECTION FOR OUR LOVE 103

WHAT'S THE NAME OF THE GAME? 111

THE UPS, DOWNS, OVERS AND UNDERS OF LOVE

1.
She must have thought I was her laundry, 'cause she really hung me out to dry.

2.
Don't give up on me, darlin', or I might start feelin' down over you.

3.
If I had it all to do over again, I think I'd ask someone to do it for me.

4.
Tryin' to get over you is startin' to get under my skin.

5.
Our love is like an old pickup truck that's been over lots of bumps in the road.

6.

It didn't take me long to get over you, 'cause time passes fast when I'm havin' fun.

7.

When you feel like things ain't goin' your way, you're probably right—they ain't.

8.

My wife always liked Roy Rogers, so she yelled "Happy Trails to You" as she kicked me out the door.

9.

If everybody loves somebody sometime, how come nobody's lovin' me right now?

10.

Call me anytime you want, but check first to make sure I'm home.

11.
I don't want nothin' to do with worn-out clothes, worn-out shoes, or worn-out men.

12.
I'm gonna call an exterminator if you don't stop buggin' me.

13.
I make money bettin' on horses, but I always lose when I bet on love.

14.
My darlin's got a very clean mind, probably because she changes it so often.

15.
Seems like every time I take you out, somebody else takes you home.

16.
Sometimes it's over before it's over, and sometimes it ain't.

17.
If life's filled with ups and downs, how come we never have any ups?

18.
Until you've seen me at my best, I sure ain't gonna show you my worst.

19.
I ain't over you yet, and that's the way it's gonna stay.

20.
You gotta learn the ins and outs of love before you can live with its ups and downs.

21.
I was just gettin' over him when he walked all over me again.

22.
He was my one and only, but I was just one of many for him.

23.
Sorry, darlin', but I ain't up to bein' put down.

24.
I ain't never, and I'm beginnin' to think I never will.

25.
I risked almost everything for love, and I ain't takin' that risk no more.

26.
He says he's a work in progress, but I ain't seen no work and I sure ain't seen no progress.

27.
I can't get over you 'til I'm done gettin' over her.

28.
He kept puttin' me down, so I packed up and left him.

29.
I won't get over her 'til the day I'm six feet under.

30.
Let me know when it's over, baby, so I can get over you.

31.
She stood me up before I could sit down.

32.
He couldn't tell which end was up even when he was standin' on his head.

33.
I don't care if her elevator don't stop on all floors, as long as it stops on mine.

34.
I don't know what's up with her, and that really puts me down.

35.
I ain't nothin' without her, but she's really somethin' without me.

36.
Hang in there, baby, 'cause I'm really hung up on you.

37.
I gave 'til it hurt before I finally gave up on him.

38.
She went out and bought a ladder, just so she could look down on me.

39.
I knew you was gonna stand me up when I saw you sittin' down with him.

40.
Things have really been lookin' up since he quit puttin' me down.

TEARS, BEERS, BARS AND DRINKIN'

41.
If you'll loan me your shoulder to cry on, I can throw all my Kleenex away.

42.
A cold beer and an armful of you make for the end of a perfect day.

43.
She's still my Margarita, even if she don't drink nothin' but beer.

44.
Her eyes sparkle in the moonlight like an empty beer can layin' beside the road.

45.
She drove me to drink 'til her car ran out of gas.

46.
I don't cry over spilt milk, but beer's another matter.

47.
Six beers are about all I can handle, 'specially when he chugs them down real fast.

48.
It seems like a six-pack is the only support group I've got right now.

49.
Seems like every time I drink a double, I start feelin' single again.

50.
I was drinkin' to forget her when I forgot what I was tryin' to forget.

51.
Killin' time with a bottle finally started killin' me.

52.
She drove me to drink 'til her car broke down.

53.
I was drinkin' a lot before I met her, and now I'm drinkin' a whole lot more.

54.
She's either uglier than I thought, or this whiskey ain't workin' no more.

55.
When the whiskey stopped tastin' bad, she started lookin' pretty good.

56.
She drank all my whiskey before she started feelin' frisky.

WHO'S LEAVIN' AND WHO'S COMIN' BACK?

57.
When the devil starts wearin' ice skates, I'll be comin' back to you.

58.
'Til my plane rolled down the runway, I didn't think I could run away from you.

59.
When the ducks head back to Minnesota, I'll be headin' home to you.

60.
Lovin' you's a tough job, honey, and I ain't tough enough for the job anymore.

61.
My wife's done run off with my best friend, and I'm hopin' it won't hurt our friendship.

62.
My troubles left me when he walked out the door.

63.
I've seen her before, and her after ain't bad either.

64.
Yes, baby, you can have it all, 'cause I'm leavin' you right now.

65.
What in tarnation is reincarnation, and when are you comin' back to me?

66.
Baby, I ain't been with you long enough to miss you when you're gone.

67.
I got home so late I backed in the door so my honey would think I was just leavin'.

68.
She didn't bother to tell me she was leavin', but that ain't botherin' me at all.

69.
I was lonely 'til he came back home, but I've been lonelier ever since.

70.
She left town with the mailman and didn't leave no forwardin' address.

71.
If it didn't hurt when she left, it wasn't meant to be.

72.
I didn't know how I'd feel when you left, but it's sure been fun findin' out.

73.
She said good things to me when I left – goodbye, good luck, and good riddance.

74.
I stuck with him for 20 years, but finally came unglued and left.

75.
She keeps goin' on about my goin' off.

76.
Seems like you're always goin' out just as I'm comin' in.

77.
Love came to stay on the day he went away.

78.
When I said hello, she was already thinkin' goodbye.

79.
He can't be makin' a comeback, 'cause he ain't never been nowhere to come back from.

80.
When I asked her to love me or leave me, she headed for the door.

81.
Her lips brought me home, and her arms kept me from leavin' again.

THE EYES HAVE IT, DARLIN'

82.
Better watch your step, darlin', 'cause love may be blind, but I sure ain't.

83.
I thought I'd seen everything until she took everything off.

84.
I really didn't see you the first time I saw you, but I'm sure seein' you now.

85.
Look at everybody all you want, but don't let me catch you lookin' at every body.

86.
We were blinded by love, but marriage opened our eyes real fast.

87.
We ain't been seein' enough of each other, baby, so why don't we turn on the lights?

88.
Don't let me catch you lookin' at her while I'm lookin' the other way.

89.
I first saw him across a smoke-filled room, and he really looked better that way.

90.
I don't know what made me see what I saw in you.

91.
My friends said she was as pretty as a picture, but I knew I'd been framed when I saw her.

92.
Always remember, darlin', that it's better to be looked over than to be overlooked.

93.
The end is in sight, and the rest of her looks pretty good, too.

94.
He don't look half bad to me, but that's about all I can see right now.

95.
I ain't gonna overlook how much you looked her over.

96.
Seein' you goin' out with her was enough to do me in.

97.

When I saw her lookin' at me, I forgot what I was tryin' to forget.

98.

The last time I saw her was the first time I'd really seen her.

99.

I saw her last, last night, but I'll see her first tonight.

100.

I was lookin' at her while she was lookin' at him, so she didn't see the look I gave her.

101

When I saw the way you looked at each other, I knew for sure he wasn't your brother.

102.
Seein' her in a low-cut dress was always an uplifting experience.

103.
I ain't been seein' much of her lately, and she just told me I'd better get used to it.

104.
There just ain't nothin' good-lookin' about an ugly man.

105.
When I first saw her, I knew they didn't make a model like that any more.

106.
I overlooked her 'til I really looked her over.

__SO, WHAT DO YOU THINK OF ME?__

107.
You should be a probation officer, baby, 'cause you're always tellin' me what I'm doin' wrong.

108.
I'm leavin' you, baby, 'cause the bigger you get, the smaller I feel.

109.
I thought I knew all about you, but I really didn't know nothin' at all.

110.
You think you're as pure as new fallen snow, but you're nothin' but road slush to me.

111.
I ain't no officer of the law, baby, but I wouldn't mind pinchin' you.

112.
If I ain't what you thought I'd be, maybe you'd better be thinkin' about somebody else.

113.
You may think you're the cat's meow, but you're just a big fur ball to me.

114.
If you don't like me the way I am, you may need to try changin' yourself.

115.
My life ain't the same without you, and I thank my lucky stars for that.

116.
You're none the worse for wear, in spite of what you're wearin' right now.

117.
Darlin', you change your mind more often than Dolly Parton changes her outfits.

118.
If you can't kiss better than that, baby, I'm gonna have to go lookin' for help.

119.
Honey, I'm gonna buy you a drum so you can stop beatin' your chest.

120.
I know a few things about you, and I really don't care about the rest.

121.
Since your needs are my needs, maybe we need to get together.

122.
I'm gonna call you my specialist, baby, 'cause there's lots that's special about you.

123.
You're the perfect man for me, darlin', 'cause you've got a smile on your face, a song in your heart, and money in your pocket.

124.
If all men are idiots, I think I married their king.

125.
I don't care if a breeze caresses the trees, as long as I'm the one caressin' you.

126.
You're too good for me, darlin', and that's really too bad.

127.
If I can't be you're #1, can I take a number and wait?

128.
I'm layin' here thinkin' about all the lies you've laid on me.

129.
I don't know what I'm doin', but doin' it with you is sure lots of fun.

130.
If I had a wish, I'd wish I had you.

131.
I knew others before you, but you're still the only one I've ever known.

132.
I've never heard of me, have you?

133.
If the devil loves sinners, he must really be in love with you.

PAY ATTENTION TO WHAT I'M TELLIN' YOU, DARLIN'

134.
Just think, darlin', in a perfect world, I would be just as perfect as you

135.
Don't go ringin' my doorbell, baby, 'cause I don't wanta waste the electricity on you.

136.
When the preacher man said to love thy neighbor, he didn't mean what you're thinkin' right now.

137.
If you lay your hand on my leg again, you're gonna be missin' four fingers and a thumb.

138.
If I ain't told you lately that I love you, maybe it's because I don't.

139.
Baby, if I was a magician, I'd be makin' myself disappear right now.

140.
When stars fell on Alabama, one of them must have hit you on the head.

141.
Remember, darlin', smokin' kills and when you're dead, you ain't no longer alive.

142.
I may like you when I get to know you, but I sure don't like you now.

143.
Darlin', please tell me when you're gonna drop the other shoe, so I can try to get out of the way.

144.
Don't try cross-dressin' around me, baby, 'cause I can only keep up with one of you at a time.

145.
I've got a lot on my mind, darlin', so please get off my back.

146.
I ain't never gonna be your dog, so you can quit pullin' my chain right now.

147.
Hang up the telephone, baby, and try talkin' to me for a change.

148.
I don't know what you're doin' to me, but please do it again real soon.

149.
Better let me out of the doghouse, darlin', before I start growlin' again.

150.
If you don't quit spendin' so much time on that computer, I'm gonna kick the dot com thing outta here.

151.
Christmas ain't even close, baby, but you're already cookin' my goose.

152.
If you really knew me, you'd know I've known no other.

153.
You won't have to tell me you're mine, if you'll tell me there ain't nobody else.

154.
You ain't no country star, baby, so don't try singin' your way into my heart.

155.
You can't make a silk purse out of a sow's ear, and you can't make a lady out of me.

156.
Tell it to me easy, honey, so it won't be so hard to take.

157.
You can't never be as good as me, 'cause you're already a whole lot better.

158.
I ain't gonna let your troubles trouble me 'til they start troublin' you.

159.
I ain't gonna be home when you call, so you don't need to call me no more.

160.
I ain't no banjo, darlin', so you'd better quit pickin' on me.

161.
If you stand me up again, baby, I'm gonna be sittin' down with somebody else.

162.
If I was a woman, I wouldn't go out with a man like me.

163.
I don't care where you lay your head, as long as I'm layin' mine beside you.

164.
Those boots stickin' out from under your bed sure as hell ain't mine.

165.
I ain't no dentist, darlin', but I can tell you're lyin' through your teeth.

166.
Talk is cheap, so talk as much as you'd like.

167.
Some things are bigger than both of us, and you're becomin' one of 'em.

168.
I'm you're woman six days a week, but I need the other day for partyin' with the girls.

169.
If we keep goin', darlin', we'll have more kids than a pair of rabbits on Viagra.

170.
Darlin', if you don't get it right, you're gonna be left.

171.
I'd rather be a nobody than somebody with no body.

172.
There ain't nothin' wrong with me that a little bit of you won't cure.

173.
I'll be anything you want me to be, as long as I can still be me.

174.
I fell for you once, darlin', and that was one time too many.

175.
To me, the state of matrimony is a "show me" state.

176.
Unless you're a gold miner, darlin', don't try stakin' a claim on me.

177.
Even if I loved you less, I'd still love you more than anyone else.

178.
Sorry, darlin', but I live in my own little world, and it ain't big enough for both of us.

179.
Darlin', why can't you love me for who I am instead of who you want me to be?

180.
You might as well get comfortable, baby, 'cause I came here to stay.

181.
You're barkin' up the wrong tree if you wanta put a collar on me.

182.
Don't do to me what you did to her, and her, and her, and her.

183.
Honk, baby, if you wanta go honky tonkin' with me.

184.
Somethin' in our relationship don't add up, so I'm subtractin' me.

BEIN' SMART, BUT LOOKIN' DUMB

185.
If I'd known then what I know now, I'd have known I didn't know nothin'.

186.
I don't wanta finish high school, 'cause then I'd be smarter than everybody I know.

187.
Just when I thought I had everything, I found out I didn't have you.

188.
A mind's a precious thing to waste, darlin', but that's somethin' you'll never have to worry about.

189.
Of all the things I don't understand, women are at the top of the list.

190.
Beethoven didn't wear boots and spurs, and you can bet your guitar on that.

191.
When all is said and done, there's really nothin' left to say or do.

192.
Sayin' men are from Mars may be givin' some of them too much credit.

193.
I learned all I know in kindergarten, just before I quit school for good.

194.
You can come home with me if you want, but I ain't sure what my husband will say when we get there.

195.
I don't mind you wearin' boxer shorts, baby, but those you got on ain't mine.

196.
Since I'm funny only half the time, I guess I'm just a half-wit to you, darlin'.

197.
She took me for a ride and didn't even have no car.

198.
I was gonna write you a letter, but I couldn't remember your name.

199.
Havin' kids may be out of the question, darlin', 'cause I sat on my spurs last night.

200.
Sorry, darlin', but that ten-gallon hat don't look good on your two-gallon head.

201
She didn't play poker, so she thought a royal flush was somethin' that happened in a bathroom.

202.
She asked my to spend the night, but I didn't have my toothbrush so I had to go home.

203.
You may be a cowboy, darlin', but you ain't wearin' them spurs to bed.

204.
I never worry about what he thinks, 'cause he don't think very often.

205.
I have everything I ever wanted except her.

206.
He blows his own horn so much, he oughta be playin' in a band.

207.
I know everything about her, except her name.

208.
She was my woman, 'til I found out she was a man.

209.
I finally put two and two together after starin' at these four walls all night.

THE BARNYARD, THE CIRCUS AND THE ZOO

210.
Go ahead and hand me a banana, darlin', 'cause you're always makin' a monkey out of me.

211.
My life's like a three-ring circus with nothin' goin' on in two of the rings.

212.
Don't come 'round the hen house tonight, darlin', 'cause the rooster's comin' home about seven.

213.
I may be goin' to the dogs, honey, but at least I ain't bein' catty like you.

214.
This is ladies night out, baby, so this chick won't be comin' home to roost.

215.
You're dog won't be hungry tonight, 'cause he just ate the seat of my pants.

216.
Chicken soup is good for the soul, but possum stew ain't half bad either.

217.
Don't tell me we hit a cow, 'cause we ain't even out of the parkin' lot yet.

218.
If I had a horse, I'd sure be ridin' herd on you.

219.
I ain't no rabbit, darlin', but I'd sure like to do some bunny hoppin' with you.

220.
Put the dog out, baby, and we'll have a doggone good time tonight.

221.
I'm gonna call you my bunny, 'cause you've really got a nice lookin' tail.

222.
I can't count my chickens before they're hatched, 'cause I still ain't learned to count.

223.
I may be a chicken, but I ain't henpecked yet.

224.
You should be a rooster, darlin', 'cause you really know how to crow.

225.
You ain't no donkey, baby, so you'd better quit actin' like an ass around me.

226.
My chicken sleeps with its head under one wing, but you can sleep under my roof.

227.
I'm feelin' so henpecked that I'm gonna sleep with the chickens tonight.

228.
Get the chickens fed early, darlin', 'cause we're goin' to town tonight.

229.
Treat your woman better than your horse or she'll be callin' you her horse's butt.

230.
Now that I've found you, baby, this old dog ain't gonna hunt no more.

231.
I ain't no mouse, darlin', so why don't you let me out of this trap?

232.
She reminds me of Mother Goose, 'cause she's always got a story to tell.

233.
You ain't no dog, mister, so you'd better stop pawin' me.

234.
Love me, love my dog, or try barkin' up another tree.

TRUCKS, TRAINS, JAILS AND PRISONS

235.
Put me in the jailhouse, honey, so I can have a good meal for a change.

236.
I was in prison when you were born, and I won't be out 'til long after you're gone.

237.
I took the train to Nashville and got my caboose kicked outta every bar in town.

238.
He came on stronger than an 18-wheeler with no brakes.

239.
Daddy's in prison, mama's on parole, and I'm goin' to jail.

240.

He's my truck drivin' baby, and he really knows how to shift my gears.

241.

He must have been a dump-truck driver, 'cause he really dumped on me.

242.

I'm doin' time, I can't get out, and it's really doin' me in.

243.

Her caboose looks a lot better than the rest of her train.

244.

He took me ridin' on a train and really blew my whistle.

SLEEPIN', DAY-DREAMIN' AND MAKIN' BELIEVE

245.
There's 24 hours in a day, but none of 'em seem to belong to me.

246.
Our old dog snores just like you, so why don't the two of you try sleepin' together.

247.
Why spend time day-dreamin' when you've already got the man of your dreams in me?

248.
I was thinkin' about you with no clothes on this morning, but then I got dressed and went to work.

249.
If you ain't gonna stop and ask for directions, just drive real slow while I take a nap.

250.
Early to bed and early to rise means you ain't got nothin' better to do.

251.
I ain't been able to sleep at night since I started day-dreamin' about you.

252.
If you don't shave your beard today, you'll be sleepin' with the dogs tonight.

253.
She was the girl of my dreams 'til I finally woke up.

254.
I've got bags under my eyes and one on the other side of the bed.

255.
I started day-dreamin' with my eyes wide open when she walked in the door.

256.
I didn't have to make believe after I learned to believe in her.

<u>WHAT YOU SEE AIN'T ALWAYS WHAT YOU GET</u>

257.
If life's a bowl full of cherries, how come I didn't get nothin' but the pits?

258.
Mama said there'd be days like this, but she didn't tell me they'd come around so often.

259.
Baby, there ain't no one better than you, as long as you don't count me.

260.
Bein' only half bad means you still ain't bein' good.

261.
I ain't got no body, but nobody seems to care.

262.
There wasn't anyone before you, and there ain't nobody now.

263.
The truth hurts, darlin', so go ahead and tell me another lie.

264.
I wanta go to heaven, but didn't know I'd have to go through hell to get there.

265.
She really thinks I'm more than I am, which means I ain't what I am to her.

266.
Our house ain't much to look at, darlin', but it's sure been a wonderful home.

267.
Until you've walked a mile in my shoes, you'll never know how much they hurt my feet.

268.
My darlin's too good to be true and that makes him false to me.

269.
If you can't be you, don't try to be me.

270.
If beauty is only skin deep, she must have really thin skin.

271.
There'll never be another like her, and I thank the Good Lord for that.

272.
Baby, my job's so bad that I feel better when I can stay home sick.

273.
What you see is what you get, if you're lucky.

274.
When he said he'd take me to Paris, I didn't know he meant Paris, Tennessee.

275.
He's a room full of sunshine and a house full of rain.

276.
When he left me standin' at the altar, I didn't know how lucky I was.

277.
I went and fell for the wrong guy while I was lookin' for "mister right."

278.
When she wore her wonder bra, it sure made everyone wonder.

279.
She was the prettiest rose in the garden, and her buds looked pretty good too.

280.
What I see in you now, I never saw before.

281.
Is you is who I think you is, or is you somebody else?

282.
I asked her to help me get rid of the blues, but she left me red-faced instead.

283.
She don't have no halo, but she's still an angel to me.

284.
She's tryin' to get by on her looks, but just don't have the face for it.

285.
Better put your make-up on, darlin', or folks won't know who you are.

286.
Somewhere over the rainbow sure ain't nowhere close to here.

287.
Bein' a somebody don't mean nothin' if nobody cares.

288.
She don't have no driver's license, but she's sure been drivin' me crazy.

289.
She must be a ventriloquist, 'cause she always speaks for me.

290.
She loved me for what I was 'til she found out that wasn't much.

291.
When everything's comin' up roses, how come I don't get nothin' but weeds?

292.
He had the looks, but he didn't have the touch.

293.
She made me what I am, which don't say much for her.

294.
After marryin' for better or worse, she got better and I got worse.

295.
She was a woman of the night tryin' to make a go of it during the day.

296.
I thought she was right for me until she left.

297.
Seems like she's always long on demand, but short on supply.

298.
She's a two-timin' woman livin' in a one-horse town.

299.
To her, a seven-course dinner meant two pieces of bread with mayo, mustard, bologna, cheese and a pickle in between.

300.
He wasn't even close to perfect, but he still looked good to me.

301.
He may not be cuckoo yet, but he's sure half-way outta the clock.

ACHES, PAINS, LOSSES AND GAINS

302.
I can't make things right for you, darlin', 'cause you've always been wrong for me.

303.
There ain't nothin' I won't do, as long as I'm doin' it with you.

304.
Stress can be caused by eatin' too much, and that really stresses me out.

305.
My man's a country singer, 'cause nobody wants him singin' in town.

306.
My in-laws have made an outlaw outta me.

307.
Money ain't everything, darlin', but it makes up for everything else you don't have.

308.
If I ain't got what it takes, baby, you're welcome to take what I've got.

309.
She said "adieu" before I could say "I do."

310.
Darlin', I'd like to be called somethin' rather than nothin' at all.

311.
Takin' you out is doin' me in.

312.
You ain't my honey no more, 'cause you're lovin' me less than ever before.

313.
She sent a lot of cowboys to their graves craven her.

314.
You can keep the ring, but please give me back my heart.

315.
She's my part-time lover and my full-time wife.

316.
I was flyin' high 'til our divorce decree clipped my wings.

317.
I forgot what I was tryin' to forget when I saw you again last night.

318.
When I asked her to line-dance with me, she put me at the end of her line.

319.
She really went down the drain when she ran off with that plumber.

320.
She's a gal for all seasons, and I pay her alimony in every one of 'em.

321.
Getting' over you was easy, 'cause there wasn't much to get over.

More Country Music for Laughin', Lovin' and Livin' It Up

322.
I only miss her seven days a week.

323.
I don't mind waitin', darlin', but I ain't waitin' on you no more.

324.
When my darlin' went to heaven, it knocked the hell right out of me.

325.
Our love went dry right after our cow and our well.

326.
The only ring I ever got from him was the one he left 'round the tub.

327.
I lost my job two weeks ago, but then my wife left me and made things a whole lot better.

328.
You were the one I wanted, but she's the one I got.

329.
Our divorce got rid of him, but it ain't got rid of the heartaches he left behind.

330.
Rememberin' where I came from is easy, but forgettin' it sure is hard.

331.
He loves himself so much that there ain't nothin' left for me.

332.
He's out doin' what I'm doin' without.

333.
She left me up the creek without a paddle, and our divorce left me there without a boat.

334.
He gave me a bad time, even in the good times.

335.
She was my #1 'til #2 came along.

336.
She didn't let go of me 'til she let me go.

337.
It ain't love if it don't hurt when you're apart.

338.
I've loved and I've yearned, and they took all the money I ever earned.

339.
Just when my heart was gettin' better, I got another "Dear John" letter.

340.
I didn't know where to go when I found out she was gone.

341.
Losin' him was terrible, but findin' him again was even worse.

342.
She was my one and only, 'cause there weren't no number two.

343.
When she said she couldn't, I knew she really meant she wouldn't.

344.
I don't have much now that he's left me, but it's a whole lot more than I had when we were together.

345.
Seems like Tennessee has everything except a girl for me.

HUNTIN', FISHIN' AND YOU

346.
If you go dove huntin' again today, I'm gonna be shootin' you a bird.

347.
I caught her while we was fishin', but only after she hooked me good.

348.
I was fishin' for love when I caught her.

349.
You can have all of me, 'cept when I'm fishin', huntin' or drinkin' with the boys.

350.
He's like an old dog that's forgot how to hunt, but still knows how to look.

351.
Now that I've found you, darlin', this old dog ain't gonna hunt no more.

352.
She told me I could either quit fishin' or kiss her bass goodbye.

353.
If you go huntin' again today, you'll be huntin' me tomorrow.

<u>GROWIN' UP, GROWIN' OUT AND GROWIN' SMARTER</u>

354.
Darlin', you're old enough to know better, but I'm sure glad you don't.

355.
It's nice knowin' folks you've known so long that you really know all about them.

356.
I still wear spurs, but there ain't much jingle left in my jangle any more.

357.
I don't hear too well, honey, so just blow in my ear to get my attention.

358.
I don't remember her name, but I sure remember everything else.

359.
They say dippin's bad for your teeth, but I ain't had no problem since mine all fell out.

360.
My baby used to shake, rattle and roll, but now he just eats, sleeps and snores.

361.
If Viagra's half as good as they say, it'll make some men half as good as they think are.

362.
The only heavy breathin' I hear anymore is mine when I walk up the stairs.

363.
I don't get around much anymore, maybe because I'm so square.

364.
Darlin', there's no one else as close to perfect as you, unless it's me.

365.
I ain't no has-been, baby, but I've sure been had before.

366.
My honey always stops to think, but then forgets why he stopped.

367.
Darlin', if I'd wanted to be a lady, I'd never have married you.

368.
As we grow older, baby, it seems like we're spendin' more time in the past lane.

369.
Tell me where you're goin', and I'll tell you where I've been.

370.
Seems like you'll do about anything, as long as you don't have to do it yourself.

371.
I've been there, done that, and I ain't gonna do it again.

372.
Take good care of your woman, and she'll take good care of you.

373.
Seems like the older I get, the better I was.

374.
I don't know what I don't know, but I do know I don't care.

375.
I got old very young after I married him.

376.
Time marches on, and it seems like I'm startin' to lead the parade.

377.
She used to look bigger comin' than goin', but now everything's turned around.

378.
He was the light of my life 'til his bulb burned out.

379.
I had to quit havin' sex at seventy, so I'm hopin' they'll raise the speed limit again real soon.

380.
It seems like the more I age, the older I get.

381.
There ain't no place I want to go where I ain't already been.

382.
They don't make 'em like her anymore, and I'm sure happy about that.

383.
She wasn't bad, but her good was a little bit tarnished.

LOVE, LOVE, LOVE

384.
I thought I'd had enough of her 'til I found out
enough just wasn't enough.

385.
All of you is all I ever wanted after all, darlin'.

386.
I've quit smokin', drinkin' and dippin', but I ain't
never gonna quit lovin' you.

387.
Love makes the world go 'round, and that's why I'm
gettin' dizzy over you.

388.
I've got a big appetite, baby, and I'm really hungry
for your love.

389.
Our love's like a piece of duct tape that's got us stuck together for life.

390.
Better get me to a doctor, baby, 'cause my heart's doin' flip-flops over you.

391.
I don't have to wait for Thanksgivin' to be thankful for havin' you.

392.
Our love had a beginning, but we ain't never gonna let it end.

393.
Just when I thought I was all over you, I started hurtin' all over again.

394.
Ain't nothin' in the world I wouldn't do, if I could just do it with you.

395.
They say there's a place for everything, so we gotta keep lookin' 'til we find a place for our love.

396.
If you say I ain't good enough for you, that's good enough for me.

397.
Won't nothin' ever come between me and you, darlin', 'cept maybe me or you.

398.
There ain't nothin' worth doin', if I ain't doin' it with you.

399.
I ain't long for this world, baby, so please don't cut short our love.

400.
You ain't the only one I've ever known, but you're the only one I've ever loved.

401.
Doin' without your love is about to do me in.

402.
Lovin' you now is better than never.

403.
It ain't no secret that I love you, darlin', so we don't have to whisper no more.

404.
Without your love, I'm like a glass of unsweet tea.

405.
There'll never be another like my dear, dear mother.

406.
He put air in my tires and love in my life.

407.
This room wasn't spinnin' 'til he came walkin' through the door.

408.
I ain't never had another, and I don't want another now.

409.
I loved too much and got too little in return.

410.
Our love must be bankrupt, 'cause there sure ain't nothin' left.

411.
Lovin' her was easy, but losin' her was hard.

412.
Man, he sure knows how to treat me like a woman.

413.
She was my only love, and I loved only her.

414.
I saw northern lights and southern stars when I fell in love with her.

415.
I love havin' his feet at the foot of my bed.

416.
When he holds me in his arms, I feel like a biscuit hot out of the oven.

417.
I'm always in good hands when I'm with him.

418.
Love without love ain't love.

419.
She taught me that love was more than sayin' I love you.

420.
Love holds us together just like a bottle of super glue

421.
She ain't no American Idol, but I still idolize her.

422.
I never loved no one like her, and I never will again.

423.
Love is love, nothin' more and nothin' less.

More Country Music for Laughin', Lovin' and Livin' It Up

424.
Nothin's certain in life, but I'm certainly in love with you.

425.
I gave her everything she wanted, except love.

426.
You'd better make sure that the one you're lovin' is the same one who's lovin' you.

427.
Love ain't love without love.

428.
Everybody loves somebody, and she's got the body I love.

<u>LAUGHIN', LOVIN' AND LIVIN' IT UP</u>

429.
Sorry, darlin', but livin' it up with you is gettin' too hard to live down.

430.
Put on some lipstick and your best perfume, 'cause we're gonna go boot-scootin' tonight.

431.
Daylight Saving Time ain't nothin' compared to the time we had last night.

432.
Baby, when the music starts playin', we gotta get up and dance.

433.
Guess I'll have to gain some weight, 'cause there just ain't enough of me to go around.

434.
Country music's good for clappin' your hands, tappin your toes, and forgettin' all about your woes.

435.
I celebrated July 4th with a 5th and was still hung over on the 6th.

436.
Doin' the cow-chip boogie keeps me watchin' where I step.

437.
I was flyin' high last night, but my darlin' grounded me today.

438.
I drank so much last night that I fell on the floor before I fell off my chair.

More Country Music for Laughin', Lovin' and Livin' It Up

439.
I spent three days with her last night.

440.
I work like hell all week, so I can play like the devil on Saturday night.

441.
Havin' a brand new man is gettin' to be old stuff with her.

442.
I ran after a lot of women 'til my darlin' taught me how to walk.

443.
I'll bring the fireworks, you bring the matches, and we'll have a blast tonight.

444.
If you'll be my woman tonight, I'll be your man in the morning.

445.
She jiggles more than Jello when she goes walkin' down the street.

446.
Tennessee Saturday nights are made for laughin', lovin' and livin' it up.

447.
I don't need no stool at the bar, 'cause I usually end up on the floor.

IT'S EITHER TOO HOT OR TOO COLD

448.
She's so frigid I had to be treated for frostbite after takin' her out last night.

449.
Where there's a will, there's supposed to be a way, but when I have the will, she says, "no way!"

450.
If wishes really came true, you'd already be where you're tellin' me to go.

451.
I've gotta let you go, darlin', 'cause my thermostat's set on hot and yours is set on cold.

452.
I'm runnin' hot and you're runnin' cold, so our love can't never be no better than lukewarm.

453.
She turned me off before I could turn her on.

454.
I was lookin' for somethin' more, but found a whole lot less.

455.
She must be part Eskimo, 'cause she's made our bedroom as cold as an igloo.

456.
When she started burnin' the biscuits, things really got hot in the kitchen.

457.
My ex-wife shorted out the electric blanket, 'cause it was so cold on her side of the bed.

THERE'S BEEN A CHANGE OF DIRECTION FOR OUR LOVE

458.
He used to call me his darlin', but now he don't call me at all.

459.
Maybe we need a compass, baby, 'cause our love sure ain't goin' in the right direction.

460.
Mama said I should be careful when pickin' a man, and I sure wish I'd listened to her.

461.
I don't know what you want me to say, so I ain't sayin' nothin' right now.

462,
I never had amnesia 'til my wife asked me where I'd been all night.

463.
My old truck can't pull but half of our doublewide, so I'm takin' my half and leavin'.

464.
If you don't fix that faucet, it's gonna turn into a big drip like you.

465.
Seems like the road less traveled is the one that comes to my house.

466.
Baby, the trouble with you is me.

467.
Darlin', we'll never be goin' in the same direction 'til we learn how to gee-haw together.

More Country Music for Laughin', Lovin' and Livin' It Up

468.
Without you, darlin', I could be me again.

469.
Baby, you can have it your way after I'm on my way.

470.
When I said love me or leave me, she headed for the door.

471.
I jumped for Jack, but he'd already fallen for Jill.

472.
If the sun don't come up in the morning, I'll be sendin' your alimony check.

473.
Darlin', when all is said and done, there's nothin' more to say and nothin' more to do.

474.
Guess we'd better take up skiin', baby, 'cause our love is goin' downhill real fast.

475.
She's an upstairs woman and I'm a downstairs man, so we always meet half-way up the stairs.

476.
I don't know where I'm goin', so I hope I'll see somethin' familiar somewhere along the way.

477.
I sent her red roses, and she sent back all the thorns.

478.
I've only cried once since he left, but I've sure been smilin' a lot.

479.
There's nothin' about her I don't like, but she don't like nothin' about me.

480.
He told me he loved me, but went and put a wedding band on someone else's hand.

481.
She was the jelly on my toast 'til that stud-muffin came along.

482.
The only time he holds me is when we're dancin', and we ain't dancin' much any more.

483.
You're doin' me wrong and that ain't right.

484.
I'm puttin' my boots on backwards so I can walk back home to you.

485.
She made me remember what I was tryin' to forget.

486.
His idea of eatin' out is havin' supper on the porch.

487.
Bein' here without you is somewhere I don't wanta be.

488.
I walked in the sunshine with her, but I'm walkin' in the rain now that she's gone.

489.
I met her at a bus stop, and she's been tellin' me to stop ever since.

490.
I can't do without her, but she's doin' fine without me.

491.
We had a beautiful wedding, but our marriage got ugly real fast.

WHAT'S THE NAME OF THE GAME?

492.
I don't know how cross-dressers can afford two wardrobes when I'm havin' trouble payin' for one.

493.
I'm gonna play magician with you, darlin', so now you see me, and now you don't.

494.
Baby, please don't sin under the apple tree with anyone else but me.

495.
There ain't no way I'm gonna play the game you're wantin' me to play.

496.
I'm gonna have to practice my baseball, 'cause I just struck out with her.

497.
I'm tired of playin' the game by your rules, darlin', so you can sleep on the couch tonight.

498.
Propogatin' rhymes with matin', and I ain't havin' none of that.

499.
If lovin' me ain't in the cards you're playin', please let me deal you another hand.

500.
I don't care whether I win or lose, as long as you play ball with me.

501.
She's like true or false questions where all the answers are false.

More Country Music for Laughin', Lovin' and Livin' It Up

502.
She should be playin professional football, 'cause I ain't scored on her yet.

503.
When she sat down to play poker, I lost my heart before the cards were dealt.

504.
I took her to a baseball game and, boy, did I strike out.

505.
She didn't play poker, but she sure loved roommate roulette.

506.
If you ain't where I think you are, you must be somewhere else.

507.
Just as I rounded third base with her, she threw me out at home.

508.
He kept throwin' passes at me 'til I finally tackled him.

509.
Seems like I'm a "table for one" person in a "table for two" world.

510.
Somethin' in our relationship don't add up, so I'm subtractin' me.

ABOUT THE AUTHOR

M. Gene Newport grew up in Albion, a small farming community in southeastern Illinois not far from the Wabash River. Indiana was on the other side of the Wabash, and northwestern Kentucky was just a few miles downstream at the junction of the Wabash and Ohio Rivers. Due to the geography of the region where he was raised, Gene was exposed to country music throughout his early years. Listening to the Grand Ole Opry was a ritual in many homes and businesses every Saturday night. In addition, Gene's hometown always seemed to have a country band that entertained at various community events. Members of those bands were not professionals, but their enthusiasm always drew appreciative audiences in a town where live entertainment was a rarity.

After graduation from high school, Gene attended Eastern Illinois University where he earned a B.S. degree in Education in 1957. Music of the *Fabulous Fifties* blared forth from nickel juke boxes in student hangouts all around the campus while Gene was pursuing his undergraduate degree. A few years later, the decade of the 60s saw new artists and new music come on the scene to satisfy the public's changing musical tastes. During those same years, Gene completed requirements for the M.S. degree in Management and the Ph.D. in Business from the University of Illinois. He then began a career in university teaching and administration that spanned more than 40 years.

During his career as a professor and administrator in three universities, Gene wrote, co-authored or edited over a dozen books in the field of management. In addition, he wrote articles published in business journals throughout the United States and abroad. Through it all, Gene kept dreaming about writing a country music book just for the fun of it. His dream was partially realized in 2001when he published *Country Music for Laughin', Lovin' and Livin' It Up*. But, Gene was still not completely satisfied and started writing another country music book almost immediately. This book, *More Country Music for Laughin', Lovin' and Livin' It Up*, is the result.

Gene and his wife, Sue, live in Birmingham, Alabama. They are retired and love to travel, in addition to spending time with their children and grandchildren. Both are also country music fans, with a preference for many of the older songs that have stood the test of time so very well.

Printed in the United States
63882LVS00001B/136-144